Slave Young, Slave Long

Slave Young, Slave Long

THE AMERICAN SLAVE EXPERIENCE

BY MEG GREENE

LERNER PUBLICATIONS COMPANY · MINNEAPOLIS

To the next generation, with love: Drew, Ben, Evan, Sissy, Abbie, Natalie, Nathan, Jordy, Nicky, Isaac, Maura, and Toby

A Word about Language
Immigrants to colonial America came from many different cultures. So too did newly arrived slaves. Over time, English became the standard American language for slaves and free citizens alike. Unlike free Americans, however, people who were slaves were forbidden to learn to read and write English. Limited to oral expression, and influenced by speech patterns from their diverse backgrounds, slaves eventually developed a language recognized by many scholars as distinct from standard English. No written form of slave language existed. In order to present slave voices in this book, the author has quoted primary sources in which slave language was transcribed in various ways. Quotes appear as they did in those sources.

Website address: www.lernerbooks.com

Library of Congress Cataloging-in-Publication Data

Greene, Meg.
     Slave young, slave long : the American slave experience / by Meg Greene.
          p. cm.
     Includes bibliographical references and index.
     Summary: Presents a social and cultural history of the American slave experience with emphasis on day to day life rather than the larger political context.
     ISBN 0-8225-1739-6 (alk. paper)
     1. Slaves—United States—Social life and customs—Juvenile literature. 2. Plantation life—United States—History—Juvenile literature. 3. Slaves—United States—Social conditions—Juvenile literature. 4. Slavery—United States—History—Juvenile literature [1. Slaves—Social life and customs. 2. Plantation life. 3. Slavery—History.] I. Title.
E443.G76 1999
973'.0496—dc21   98-24109

Manufactured in the United States of America
1 2 3 4 5 6 – JR – 04 03 02 01 00 99

Contents

BEFORE THE PILGRIMS

*Your country? How came it
    yours?
Before the Pilgrims landed we
    were here.*
        —W. E. B. Du Bois,
        African-American educator

Young Ottobah Cugoano and his cousins were chasing birds and picking fruit. Suddenly, a group of men with pistols and cutlasses surrounded them. The frightened children were then marched off with the strangers.

Ottobah's captors eventually took him to a trading post along the African coast, where Ottobah saw white men for the first time. When Ottobah asked why he had been brought there, a trader told him, "To learn the ways of the *browfow,* that is the white-faced people."

Three days later, with the "rattling of chains, smacking of whips, and the groans and cries" of other captives in his ears, Ottobah watched the coastline of Africa disappear into the night. He had been loaded onto a slave ship bound for the New World—a young boy traded for a gun, a piece of cloth, and some lead.

The slave trade flourished in the American colonies in the mid-1600s.

THE FIRST ARRIVALS

"About the latter end of August [1619]," wrote John Rolfe to his friend Sir Edwin Sandys, "a Dutch man of Warr...[arrived] at Point-Comfort.... He brought not any thing but 20 and odd Negroes, w[hich] the Governor and Cape Merchant bought." The official secretary and recorder of the colony of Virginia, Rolfe did not realize that his letter marked the beginning of black history in British North America.

Little is known of the Africans who came to the British North American colonies in 1619 (one year before the Pilgrims arrived on the *Mayflower*). Surviving records do show that two of the first arrivals, known only as Antoney and Isabella, were sent to the plantation of Captain William Tucker of Kecoughtan near Elizabeth City, Virginia. The two later married. In 1623 or 1624, Isabella gave birth to the first black child born in America. The child, named William after their master, was taken to Jamestown and christened.

Until this time, indentured servants had met the labor needs of the colonists in British North America. The typical indentured servant was young, white, and male, though some women did come to the colonies. In exchange for passage to America, and the promise of food and shelter upon arrival, these immigrants agreed to work for a master for four to seven years. When the period of servitude ended, the laborer was free.

Though the first black arrivals were sold into slavery, they were treated more like indentured servants than like slaves. By performing

Slaves in colonial times could work to earn their freedom.

extra work for the master or his neighbors, some slaves earned enough money to purchase their freedom. Once free, they bought land and mingled with whites. Some free blacks even bought their own slaves, who continued to arrive with increasing regularity from Africa.

One such freed African was Anthony Johnson, who rose from slavery to become a prominent member of Chesapeake society. Arriving in Virginia in 1621, "Antonio a Negro," as he was known, was sold to work on a local tobacco plantation. Sometime during the 1630s, Anthony and his wife, Mary, gained their freedom, probably through self-purchase. Taking the last name Johnson, the couple moved to Northampton County on the Eastern Shore of Virginia. There, Anthony bought 250 acres and began to grow tobacco and raise cattle, horses, and hogs. For help, he hired white indentured servants and owned at least one slave, a black man named Casor.

By the time of Anthony's death, he had established himself as a prosperous landowner, "the Patriarch of Pungoteague Creek." Other blacks also rose from slavery to become free men and women who participated fully in their communities. In many places in colonial North America, free blacks could take out loans, sue whites in court, and serve on juries. They paid taxes and, in some colonies, voted and held minor public offices. Free blacks were often recognized by law and custom as equal to white people.

By the late 17th century, however, the opportunities that had been available to Anthony Johnson and the first generation of blacks were rapidly disappearing. No longer was the dream of having "myne owne ground [to] work when I please and play when I please" possible for them.

A variety of changes doomed slaves' hopes for freedom. The demand for American tobacco grew, yet numbers of white indentured servants began to decline. Planters thought about enslaving the native peoples of the region, but Native Americans had already proven unsuitable as workers. They were not used to hard agricultural work. In addition, Native Americans lacked immunity to smallpox and many other diseases that whites brought from Europe. As a result, they were often too ill to work. That left Africans as the most available and affordable source of labor.

"SERVICE FOR LIFE"

For planters, black slaves had several advantages over white indentured servants. While indentured servants were bound for only a few years, slaves were bound for life. The color of their skin made blacks highly visible—so they were easy to identify as slaves. Indentured servants, mostly Englishmen, had rights under English law and could appeal to the king to protect them. Black slaves had no king to protect them, and no rights that American masters were required to respect.

Finally, the supply seemed endless. African slaves had long worked on the sugar plantations of the Caribbean Islands and could be purchased from planters there. Alternately, planters could buy African slaves from both English and Dutch traders.

By the late 17th century, as the number of slaves rose, many North American colonies began to pass laws that stripped blacks of rights they had formerly enjoyed. These laws defined the differences between servants and slaves, differences based largely on the color of their skin. Robert Beverley, one of the wealthiest planters in Virginia, wrote that "slaves are the negroes . . . their servitude . . . is for life."

In Virginia, a law passed in 1662 declared that children born of a servant "negro woman . . . [shall be] held bond." Two years later, a law passed in Maryland introduced the phrase *durante vita*—"service for life"— which applied only to blacks. By the end of the century, Africans arriving in America had little hope of ever attaining freedom.

"THE SOUL-DESTROYERS"

Along the Guinea Coast in West Africa, the complicated process of buying and selling slaves began. Europeans from many countries—England, France, Portugal, and the Netherlands—built a series of forts and "factories," or trading posts, to conduct this business. Each had a "Negroe House," a dungeon for captive Africans. "As the slaves come down . . . from the inland country," trader John Barbot wrote, "they are put into a booth or prison."

The slave-trading area ran for almost 3,000 miles along the West African coast. Captives came from many tribes—Mandingo, Yoruba, Ibo, Fantins, Binis, Senegalese, and others—and from all walks of life. They were farmers, warriors, chieftains, priests, mothers, fathers, and children. "I think I was between two and three years old when the soul-destroyers tore me from my mother's arms," remembered a South Carolina slave named James Bradley. "All the way I looked back and cried." Another captive, known only as Mr. Johnson, remembered being snatched from the bushes while gathering figs.

Some Africans were kidnapped by European or Arab traders; others were taken by fellow Africans. Tribes sometimes sold lawbreakers or prisoners of war to slave traders as punishment. European merchants joked that one African could sell another into slavery, then be captured and sold himself. A popular story told of an African who sold a large number of slaves and then celebrated the transaction by having too much to drink. He awoke the next day to find himself on the same ship to America as his victims.

Slave traders conducted negotiations with "dash," or presents. Cloth, guns, trinkets, beads, blankets, food, rum, brandy, and whiskey were bartered for men, women, and children. A woman might be bought for a gallon of brandy and a handful of beads. A man's worth might amount to a wicker bottle, 2 cases of whiskey, 8 guns, and 28 blankets. Traders also used cash. During the mid-1700s, a healthy young man sold for L20 sterling, or about $90.

A TRADE IN BODIES

Captives endured a long, torturous journey to the coast. Bound and shackled, they were escorted by guards armed with guns and whips. At night they were herded into pens like animals. They were fed little, only small amounts of corn, millet, apples, or yams. Historians

Above, *African people ensnared by slave traders.* **Below,** *physical inspection at a trading station.*

estimate that only two of every five prisoners survived the journey to the African coast.

In 1795, a Scottish physician, Mungo Park, traveled to the coast with an Arab slave caravan. Some of the prisoners had been held in irons for almost three years. Park wrote:

> [The slaves] are commonly secured, by putting the right leg of one, and the left leg of another, into the same pair of fetters [chains]. By supporting the fetters with a string, they can walk very slowly. Every four slaves are likewise fastened together by the necks, . . . and in the night an additional pair of fetters is put on their hands, and sometimes a light iron chain passed around their necks.

At the trading station, captives underwent physical inspection and branding. One witness noted how prisoners were brought "into a large plain, where the surgeons examine every part . . . of them . . . men and women being all stark naked. [The] good and sound are set on one side. . . . These being so set aside . . . [are] marked on the breast with a red-hot iron, imprinting the mark of the French, English or Dutch companies . . . care is taken that the women . . . be not burnt too hard."

Branded and chained, prisoners were carried in small boats to waiting ships called slavers. These were usually 50-ton schooners, modified to carry human cargo.

Some captives never made it to the ships. Many were so distraught, recalled one trader, that they "leap'd out of the canoes . . . into the sea, and kept under water till they were drowned."

THE MIDDLE PASSAGE

The journey to the New World, known as the Middle Passage, was part of a larger commercial trade route. In return for goods such as fish and lumber from the colonies, or rum and molasses from the West Indies, ships brought slaves to America.

An average slaver carried a crew of 6 to 10 men and held from 100 to 200 slaves, though some captains crowded more on board.

"Human cargo" was often carried in small boats to slavers anchored offshore.

The voyage could take between three weeks and three months. Men, women, and children were tightly packed in the ship's hold. The air was foul and the stench suffocating. Forced into spaces no more than 18 inches high, and often chained by the neck and legs, the captives could scarcely move. "The shrieks of the women, and the groans of the dying rendered the whole a scene of horror almost inconceivable," wrote Olaudah Equiano, a captured African prince.

In good weather, slaves were let out of the hold twice a day—at 10 in the morning and 4 in the afternoon—for meals and exercise. Meals were usually cooked in big copper kettles on deck and often consisted of boiled rice, cornmeal, or yams—foods familiar to the captives. A European dish, horsebeans cooked to a mush, was another typical meal—and one that most slaves detested.

Rations were pitifully small, and malnourishment contributed to countless slave deaths. Crews sometimes used food to torment the Africans further. Olaudah Equiano described one instance:

> One day they had taken a number of fishes; and when they had killed and satisfied themselves . . . to our astonishment . . . rather than give any of them to us to eat, as we expected, they tossed the remaining fish into the sea again, although we begged and prayed for some.

Millions of captured African people died of hunger and disease on slave ships.

Disease added to the death toll. Smallpox and dysentery were rampant on most slave ships, often killing crew and "cargo" alike.

"FIXED MELANCHOLY"

Many Africans, refusing to accept enslavement, suffered from a condition the traders called "fixed melancholy." They stopped eating and drinking and eventually died. Those slaves who sought a quicker death jumped into the sea and drowned. A letter published in the *Boston Weekly News* in 1737 described a mass suicide:

> On the 14th of March we found a great deal of Discontent among the Slaves, particularly the Men, which continued till the 16th about Five o'clock in the Evening, when to our great Amazement about an hundred Men Slaves jump'd over board . . . [they] would not endeavor to save themselves, but resolv'd to die, and sunk directly down.

Another observer noted the suffering of slaves in the hold: "The sense of misery and suffocation was so terrible in the 'tween decks . . . that the slaves . . . would go mad before dying or suffocating. In their frenzy some killed others in the hope of . . . [getting] more room to breathe. Men strangled those next to them."

It was also common to find a living slave chained to one who had died. Many traders commented that they threw so many dead bodies into the sea that sharks followed the ships from Africa all the way to America.

Rebellion was a constant threat. From 1699 to 1845, slavers had more than 150 mutinies, with slaves taking control of ships, often killing their captors and trying to sail back home. Rebellion became so common that many ships in the Atlantic slave trade needed a new type of insurance called "insurrection insurance."

Mutiny by prisoners was a constant threat on slave ships.

Fewer than half the slaves shipped to America ever became effective workers. The majority died en route or were permanently crippled or weakened from the voyage. Ships were lost at sea, captured by pirates, and ravaged by disease.

Despite these perils, the slave trade flourished, and slave merchants cleared huge profits. Although precise numbers are hard to pinpoint, historians estimate that by 1807 more than 9.5 million Africans had been imported as slaves to the New World.

THE SLAVE MARKET

Almost immediately after ships docked, new terrors awaited the captives. The survivors of the Middle Passage now faced the auction block—to be sold to the highest bidder. Eager merchants and planters carefully examined the slaves to make sure they were free of disease or any other kind of physical defect. Olaudah Equiano recalled that "there was much dread and trembling among us, and nothing but bitter cries." Some slaves even feared that whites were preparing to eat them.

Slaves were sold in a variety of places—taverns, stores, warehouses, and open-air markets—and by a variety of methods. Olaudah Equiano described one type of slave auction, known as the "shout" or "scramble":

> On a signal given (as the beat of a drum) the buyers rush at once into the yard where the slaves are confined, and make choice of that parcel they like best. The noise and clamor...and the eagerness...of the buyers... increase the apprehensions of the terrified Africans.... In this manner...are relations and friends separated, most of them never to see each other again.

There was even something of a mail-order business in slaves. One planter noted, "I wrote Mr. Salmon of Barbadoes to send me a negro." Virginia planter William Fitzhugh instructed his agent to "purchase what likely Negroes you can...1, 2, 3, 4, 5, or 6 what boys and men you possibly can, as few women as may be...to

A slave auction taking place near a tavern in colonial times. Such auctions continued for more than 200 years.

purchase neither man nor woman above thirty years old." Some merchants "displayed" slaves in their homes, where potential buyers could come and inspect them.

Slaves could be purchased with small down payments, and traders offered credit on "reasonable terms" to finance the remaining cost. An advertisement in 1726 offered buyers "3, 6, 9, or 12 months credit." Prices fluctuated. In 1754, future president George Washington bought a male slave for $260.

With as many as 200 slave markets, New Orleans was known as the "Mistress of the Slave Trade." Along the main streets were slave showrooms, show windows, and depots. Fredrika Bremer, visiting New Orleans in 1850, saw a woman and child sold for $700, a girl for $350, and a young mulatto (mixed-race) man for $600. In another transaction, a "prime" field hand sold for $1,800 and a blacksmith for $2,500. A particularly beautiful girl brought the extraordinary sum of $5,000.

Landscape architect Frederick Law Olmsted, traveling through the South in 1853, took note of 22 slaves waiting in New Orleans for the boat that would take them to their new master. "Louisiana or Texas," Olmsted wrote in *The Cotton Kingdom,* " . . . pays Virginia twenty odd thousand dollars for that lot of bone and muscle."

For the newly purchased slaves, now separated forever from homes, families, and friends, life in America promised to be lonely and hard. Not long after arriving at the Virginia plantation where he was to live, Olaudah Equiano recalled that "I was now exceedingly miserable. . . . I had no person to speak [to] that I could understand. . . . I was constantly grieving and pining . . . wishing for death, rather than anything else."

GOD SEND SUNDAY

Come Day, Go Day,
God Send Sunday.

         —Slave saying

Isaac Jefferson's mother, Ursula, was a pastry cook and washerwoman. His father, George, was a field hand. In his *Memoirs of a Monticello Slave,* Isaac recalled how, as a child, he helped his mother in the kitchen and laundry—toting wood, building fires, and carrying baskets of clothing.

Many of the daily needs, and some of the luxuries, of Isaac's master, future president Thomas Jefferson, were provided through the labor of slaves. Every morning Jefferson's clothes were laid out by his body servant, Jim Hemings. Jefferson's food came from fields and gardens tended by slaves. Sukey, his cook, prepared his meals. His carriage was made by another slave, Davey Watson, and driven by two more, Jupiter and John. Jefferson's beloved home, Monticello, had been built with slave labor. Slaves were essential to the operation of the household.

Mary Anderson, a slave in Wake County, North Carolina, remembered that the plantation on which she lived had "about two hundred acres of cleared land" with a "grist mill, tannery, shoe shop, blacksmith shop, and looms for weaving cloth." Henry James Trentham, who grew up on a plantation with more than 400 slaves, boasted that his master's plantation had so many slave houses that it "looked like a small town, and there was grist mills for corn, cotton gin, shoe shops, tanning yards, and lots of looms." The plantation operated almost like a self-sufficient rural village.

Such large plantations were rare, however. Of the nearly 400,000 Southern slaveholders in 1860, more than half owned 4 slaves or fewer. Only a small number of planters—approximately 20 percent—owned 10 to 30 slaves. An even smaller number—less than 1 percent—held 50 or more slaves. One exceptional planter owned close to a thousand.

Slaves on large plantations could not help but feel occasional pride in belonging to the finest white families in the South. By contrast, slaves who worked for poorer masters were often ashamed of them. "It was considered . . . bad enough to be a slave," wrote one runaway, "but to be a poor man's slave was deemed a disgrace indeed!"

"BELLS AND HORNS"

James Henry Hammond of South Carolina left explicit instructions for the operation of his plantation: "The Overseer must see that all the negroes leave their houses in the morning," Hammond insisted, and "the negroes must be made to obey & work."

Like Hammond, most plantation owners employed strict work regimens. They used noisemakers to call slaves to and from their labor. Former slave Charley Williams recalled that his life was dictated by "bells and horns! Bells for this and horns for that! All we knowed was go and come by the bells and horns!" Williams elaborated:

> You can hear an old bell donging away on some plantation a mile or two off . . . then more bells at other places and maybe a horn . . . pretty soon . . . Old Master's old ram horn with a long toot and then some short toots, and [then] the overseer down the row of cabins, hollering right and left.

The slaves' workday commonly began at four in the morning. Some 30 minutes later, after eating breakfast, slaves were on their way to the fields. A few lashes from the overseer's whip moved stragglers and late sleepers on their way. One observer recalled seeing slave women running "with their shoes and their stockings in their hands, and a petticoat over their shoulders, to dress in the fields."

Slaves worked nonstop through the morning. The overseer, armed with a pistol and knife, mounted on horseback, and often accompanied by a vicious dog, made sure the slaves kept to their work.

At noon, they paused to eat. The length of the mealtime varied from plantation to plantation. In his memoirs, *Twenty Years a Slave*, Solomon Northup described the noon meal as "ten or fifteen minutes . . . to swallow [the] allowance of cold bacon." Ria Sorrell, by contrast, enjoyed a "rest spell at twelve o'clock of two hours." Elias Thomas's master in North Carolina gave his slaves "one hour and half."

The workday often did not end until darkness made it impossible for the slaves to continue. "The fields stretched from one end of the earth to the other," recalled one slave. Others joked that the workday went from "can [see] to can't [see]." All slaves looked forward to Sunday, their one day off.

"SLAVE YOUNG, SLAVE LONG"

The duties of field slaves varied with the time of year. During spring and summer, they cleared new land for planting rice, sugarcane, cotton, corn, or tobacco. Men and women shared the work of grubbing (digging up roots) and hoeing.

Once the fields were prepared and planted, slaves tended crops through the summer. They removed pests such as worms and boll

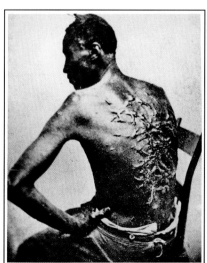

Above, *an overseer supervised slaves at work.* **Below,** *this well-known photograph shows one man's scarred back—evidence of many whippings.*

weevils from the plants by hand. To irrigate the crops, slaves carried water to the fields in buckets.

After the harvest, during fall and winter, slaves mended fences, cut down trees, built dikes, butchered pigs, and smoked the meat to make ham and bacon. Only bad weather kept slaves from working outdoors. Former North Carolina slave Jacob Manson joked during an interview: "[We] watched the weather in slavery time."

Even the youngest members of this slave family toiled in the cotton fields.

From the time children could walk, they worked at a variety of tasks, including milking cows, feeding chickens, and tending other livestock. They formed "trash gangs" that weeded and cleaned up yards. They also brought water to the field hands. One slave recalled:

> Children had to go to the fiel' at the age of six on our place. Maybe they don't do nothin' but pick up stones or tote water, but they got used to bein' there. Uncle Zack . . . lookin' at the children goin' to the field and mutter, "Slave young, slave long."

Elderly slaves who could no longer work in the fields were given other chores. They tended babies and the sick, mended clothes, or worked small vegetable gardens. Some served as midwives, folk healers, or preachers.

Some old slaves waited until their masters granted their retirement. Others, like one old man, simply announced it: "Jus' come to tell you Massa, that I've labored for you forty years now. And I done earned my keep. You can sell me, lash me, or kill me. I ain't caring which but you can't make me work no more."

"All right Jake," the master replied. "I'm retiring you, but for God's sake don't say anything to the other[s]."

Some slaves were allowed to retire when they grew old. Others labored all their lives.

"THE MOST IMPORTANT NEGRO"

On almost all large plantations, a white overseer monitored the activities of the slaves. But the actual supervising of the field hands was done by a black slave driver, so called because he "drove" slaves to work. The driver was responsible for maintaining order in the slave quarters and had the power to punish slaves when necessary. A plantation manual found among the papers of James Henry Hammond described the driver as:

> The most important negro on the plantation. He is to be treated with more respect than any other negro by both master and overseer. He is on no occasion to be treated with any indignation calculated to lose the respect of other negroes. . . . He is required to maintain proper discipline at all times; to see that no negro idles or does bad work.

The driver may have been a valued worker to the master, but many of his fellow slaves feared and hated him. Some drivers abused their

A slave driver headed a column of field hands.

power and beat or whipped the slaves. A slave woman from South Carolina, Jane Johnson, remembered her driver as "De meanest man, white or black, I ever see." Gus Feaster said his former driver "never had no quality in him a-tall, no sir-ee." Henry Cheatham was so angered by "de meanest devil dat ever lived" that he vowed to kill him "if it was de last thing I ever done."

Other drivers tried to protect the slaves. Sometimes a driver might look the other way if a stronger slave helped a weaker one in the fields. Still others ignored curfew, allowing slaves to visit with each other, or to attend forbidden parties or prayer meetings late into the night.

THE PRIVILEGED CLASS

Another important group of slaves were mechanics and craftsmen, men largely responsible for the construction and maintenance of plantation buildings and machinery. This group included master carpenters, millwrights, engineers, and blacksmiths. They often enjoyed a greater degree of freedom than other slaves, and on occasion earned money doing extra work for their masters or other slaveholders in the neighborhood.

Masters often boasted of training and "civilizing" these men. But, in truth, many of them had brought their skills from Africa. Such slaves demonstrated a high degree of technical knowledge, as their workmanship revealed. J. D. Smith, a white engineer who learned his trade from a slave, declared:

> One only need to go down South and examine hundreds of old Southern mansions, and splendid old church edifices to . . . be convinced of . . . the cleverness of the Negro artisans, who constructed nine-tenths of them.

THE SLAVE ELITE

A small number of slaves were trained to work directly for the planter's family in the "Big House." Men usually acted as butlers or valets to the master. Women were cooks, seamstresses, maids, and nannies. Children ran errands and helped in the kitchen.

A woman acting as a "mammy" often spent more time with her master's children than with her own.

Perhaps the most important black presence in the plantation household was the "mammy." She raised the white children and served as the mistress's "executive officer" in the daily running of the household. "She was the first to receive us from the doctor's hands," wrote Lewis Blair in 1889. "We saw as much of the mammy as the mother, perhaps more, and we loved her quite as well."

To both whites and blacks, the mammy was a respected figure. Lindey Faucette of North Carolina remembered her grandmother, Mammie Beckie, "who toted de keys," as a woman "whose word was law" with "Marse John and Mis Annie." Ellen Botts of Louisiana recalled that the slaves on her plantation "have to stoop to Aunt Rachel like they curtsey to Missy [the mistress]."

Slaves were often taken to the Big House as children and trained for positions they would keep for the rest of their lives. Sarah Debro remembered:

> I was kept at the big house to wait on Miss Polly. . . .
> Whenever she seed a child down in the quarters that she
> wanted to raise . . . she took them . . . and trained them. I
> was to be a housemaid. . . . I toted Miss Polly's bag and bun-
> dles, and if she dropped her handkerchief, I picked it up.

Isaac Johnson recalled that as a child his chores included "minding the table," while Madison Jefferson's jobs included "clean[ing] shoes, carrying wood, and various household duties." Katie Phoenix had to sleep on her mistress's floor at night, as "Mrs. Harris . . . was scared to be alone, asleep." One of John Smith's many jobs was "scratchin' Master's head so he could sleep . . . an' washin' Missus' feet at night 'fore she went to bed." Other slave children fanned masters and mistresses to keep them cool and keep away insects.

Like adults, slave children were subject to harsh punishments. Failure to perform their duties satisfactorily resulted in ear pinchings, hair pullings, beatings, and whippings administered by the master or mistress. Rebecca Grant remembered being whipped by her mistress when she was eight years old. Grant had failed to address the

A master and mistress greeted a slave girl who had come to bring them a gift at Christmas.

mistress's son as "Marse Henry." "Marse Henry was just a little boy," she said in an interview many years later. "[He] come 'bout halfway up to me. She wanted me to say 'Massa' to him—a baby!"

PEOPLE OF BOTH WORLDS

There were benefits to working in the house. Food cooked for the master often made its way to the house slave's table, and house slaves received secondhand clothing from the master's family. Because of their training and polish, house slaves were not easily replaced. As a result, masters and mistresses might tolerate occasional temper tantrums and rude behavior from house slaves that would have brought swift punishment to others.

House slaves were often viewed as members of the master's family and were treated more kindly than other slaves. Eliza Carmichael of Georgia understood when friends canceled a visit so they could take care of a sick house servant. Eliza Magruder of Mississippi read to her house slaves every afternoon. Isaac Hilliard of Arkansas walked to church every Sunday, so that his coachman could enjoy his "holy day" too.

But unlike field slaves, who had ample opportunities to be away from whites, house slaves were under almost constant supervision. Lewis Clarke believed that he and other house slaves were much worse off:

> We were constantly exposed to the whims and passions of every member of the family; from the least to the great their anger was wreaked upon us. Nor was our life an easy one. . . . We were always required to sit up until all the family had retired; then we must be up at early dawn in summer, and before day in winter.

Given the choice, most field hands would never work in the Big House. "We could talk and do anything we wanted," one field slave explained, "just so we picked the cotton."

More than any other slaves, house servants walked between two worlds—white and black. They brought to the white household many

A butler left slave quarters to go to work at the "Big House."

aspects of African-American culture. White families bragged about their cook's expertise with exotic spices. Planter children grew up hearing African-American folktales from their mammies.

Conversely, house servants took to the slave quarters the master's religion, manners, and language. Because of their responsibilities, they were seen as elite members of the slave community. Perhaps most important, they supplied information about the world beyond the plantation to their fellow slaves.

"NOT WEARY YET"

Harvest season routinely increased working hours for slaves. On Louisiana sugar plantations, slaves worked 18-hour days during the harvest. Some sugar factories ran in shifts, 24 hours a day, seven days a week. During the cotton harvest, men sometimes ginned until late at night. Plantation work, while changing with the seasons, was unending.

Masters devised a variety of ways to keep the slaves at work. They could always resort to threats or punishments. But the more humane, sensible, and ingenious slaveholders adopted other measures. Many planters gave slaves small amounts of money as an incentive. Bennet H. Barlow of Louisiana offered dinners, holidays, extra rations of whiskey, cash bonuses, and other gifts to reward exceptional work. Thomas Dabney of Hinds County, Mississippi, gave a few cents to his most productive cotton pickers and lesser prizes to others who worked diligently. In Perry County, Alabama, Hugh Davis divided his slaves into teams that competed for prizes.

These tokens might have impressed the slaves somewhat. But the opportunity to work with each other also provided motivation. Sam Colquitt of Alabama explained the appeal of corn shucking:

> Next to our dances, de most fun was corn-shucking. Marsa would have de corn hauled up to de crib, and piled as [high as] a house. Den he would invite de hands 'round to come and [help] shuck it. Us had two leaders ... and choose up sides. Den us see which side would win first and holler and sing. . . . Den dey sho' could work and dat pile's just vanish.

Robert Shepard of Kentucky echoed Colquitt's description:

> Dem corn shuckin's was sure 'nough big times. When us got all de corn gathered up and put in great long piles, den de gettin' ready started. Why dem womans cooked for days, and de mens would get de shoats ready to barbecue. Master would send us out to get de slaves from de farms round about dere. De place was all lit up with light-wood knot torches and bonfires, and dere was 'citement aplenty when all . . . get to singin' and shoutin' as dey made de shucks fly.

Hog killing and logrolling almost rivaled corn shucking as grand occasions. Cotton picking was another matter. Because cotton had to be harvested quickly, one former slave recalled, "Dere wasn't so much foolishness at cotton pickin' time."

Occasionally, slaves from neighboring plantations were "loaned out" to help one another. After the work was finished, slaves sat down to dinner, sometimes followed by a dance. As Gus Brown described it: "We all got together and had regular good time."

"WE DONE HAD OUR DANCE"

Many plantation owners worked their slaves only half a day on Saturdays. Though the slaves did not work Saturday afternoon for the master, the workday was far from done. Sometime between late Saturday morning and three in the afternoon, slave men and women returned home to catch up on their own chores. Men hunted, fished, worked in the garden, or earned extra money doing odd jobs for the master. Women cleaned house, did laundry, mended clothes, and cooked—especially preparing Sunday dinner.

Saturday night parties were a weekly event on many plantations. The master might contribute a hog or some chickens to barbecue, as well as some whiskey. Although some masters and their families attended the party to look on, many simply left the slaves alone to enjoy themselves.

Get-togethers often attracted slaves from other plantations. Judge Bay of South Carolina remarked: "The strictest watching could not at times prevent them from visiting their acquaintances." Other masters complained that such visits made their slaves "very impudent" and difficult to discipline. Some, such as B. McBride, refused to let slaves leave at all. He roared, "All [dealings] with negroes of other plantations is strictly forbidden."

Many masters imposed a nine o'clock curfew to keep slaves at home on Saturday nights, but with little success. The overseer, whose job was to account for the whereabouts of the slaves, rarely visited the quarters more than once a night. In some cases, overseers even joined the celebration.

Parties were filled with song and dance. Some slaves borrowed fiddles and banjos from the master. Others bought their own instruments with earnings from garden produce or odd jobs. Wash Wilson described another method:

> There wasn't no musical instruments. Us take pieces of sheep's rib or cow's jaw or a piece of iron, with an old kettle or a hollow gourd and some horsehair to make the drum. Sometime's they'd git a piece of tree trunk and hollow it out and stretch a goat's or sheep's skin over it for the drum. . . . They'd take the buffalo horn and scrape it out to make the flute.

"Whoopee, didn' us have good Sa'dd'y night frolics and jubilees," recalled one former slave. "Some clap and play de fiddle, and, man, dey danced most all night."

"DE BIG TIMES"

At Christmas, most masters provided a three-day holiday. Some planters gave five days off. Other masters let a burning log determine the length of the Christmas holiday. This practice sent slaves carefully searching for the biggest and slowest burning log to be had.

Christmas was extra-special for the children—both black and white. One slave recalled:

> Christmas was de time o'all times on dat old plantation . . . . Every child brought a stockin' up to de Big House to be filled. Dey all wanted o'de mistis stockin's 'cause now she weighed nigh on to three hundred pounds. Candy and presents was put in piles for everyone. When de names was called dey walked up and got it.

Homemade firecrackers capped off the celebration. Hogs' bladders were blown up like balloons, tied, and then thrown into a fire, where they popped to everyone's delight.

"De Han's celebrated ever' holiday dat deir white folks celebrated," stated William Henry Towns. These included Thanksgiving, Easter,

A day off sometimes meant barbecues and dancing.

birthdays for both slaves and members of the master's family, and even the return of the master from a trip. All were cause for celebration.

Perhaps the most unusual holiday for the slaves was the Fourth of July, often recognized as "de biggest day to blacks and whites." As on other special occasions, slaves got the day off to attend barbecues and dances. But this holiday was different. It was one of the few times that slaves heard political speeches—and words such as freedom, independence, and revolution.

YOUR GREAT DEATHLESS HEARTS

O, where has mother gone, papa?
What makes you look so sad?
Why sit you here alone, papa?
Has anyone made you mad?
O, tell me, dear papa.
Has master punished you again?
Shall I go bring the salt, papa,
To rub your back and cure the
pain?

—Former slave
W. H. Robinson, 1913

Lord hasten the time when these children shall be free men and women," prayed Jacob Stroyer's father. As a boy, Jacob did not understand the meaning of his father's prayer, and he resented the strict discipline that his parents enforced at home.

But when, as a young man, Jacob endured regular beatings by his master's horse trainer, he began to realize why his parents had been so cautious, so strict, and so prayerful. Like all slave parents, Jacob's mother and father could not protect him. Although he was their son, they could not raise him as they saw fit. Jacob belonged to his master.

THE SLAVE CODES

Slaves had no legal rights. They were not allowed to leave the plantation without permission. They were not allowed to learn to read or write. Slave marriages were not recognized by law. These restrictions were spelled out throughout the South in laws called slave codes. The codes gave masters complete control over their "property."

Even family life was regulated. In his "Rules for the Plantation," Mississippi planter William Ervin set out these instructions:

> Each family to live in their own house. The husband to provide firewood and see that they are all provided for and wait on his wife. The wife to cook & wash for the husband and her children and attend to the mending of clothes. Failure on either part . . . must be corrected by words first but if not reformed to be corrected by the Whip.

Many owners developed elaborate systems of patrols to track down runaways and rule breakers. The patrollers, or "paddyrollers" as the slaves called them, were often poor whites hired by the planters. They were armed and assisted by trained bloodhounds, which slaves often feared more than the patrollers themselves.

BY ANY OTHER NAME

The master's authority touched every aspect of daily life. Masters even named slaves and their children. Slaves newly arrived from Africa often found themselves with new Christian names, such as John or Sarah, or classical names such as Caesar, Cato, or Pompey. Slaves commonly took the master's family name.

Slaves didn't always adopt their new names willingly. William Wells Brown remembered "losing" his name as a young boy. When the master's nephew, also named William, arrived to live at the plantation, Brown was ordered to change his name out of respect for the nephew. When he refused, "I received several whippings for telling people my name was William, after orders were given to change it."

When James Henry Hammond purchased eight-year-old Sam Jones in the early 1830s, he changed the boy's name to Wesley. Nearly 30 years later, when Wesley, still a slave on Hammond's plantation, became a father, he named his son Sam Jones.

Another slave boy met a Georgia planter and his son out walking. The planter greeted the boy, saying, "Howdy, John." The small child replied, "My name is Norman." "Ah, yes Norman," repeated the planter. As the planter and his son continued their walk, they overheard someone asking Norman who the old man was. "I don't know who he is," said Norman, *"but he know me."*

Some masters did allow slave parents to name their children. The names the slaves chose often sounded strange to white ears, because they had African origins. A child might be named after a day or a month, or for a particular trait that parents wished to instill. The name Quack meant *Quaco*—a male born on Wednesday. Squash was a female born on Sunday; Phibbi, a female born on Friday. In time, many such African names became Americanized. Quack became Jacco or Jack. Phibbi became Phoebe.

BROTHERS AND SISTERS

Until slave children were old enough to work, most enjoyed many of the same kinds of play and adventures as white children. Slave children often played with the master's children. Together they might roam the plantation, hunt, fish, pick berries, or play games.

"I knew no difference between myself and the white children, nor did they seem to know any in turn," wrote Lunceford Lane. Sam Aleckson remembered that until he was ten years old, "it had never dawned on me that my condition was not as good as any other boy in the country." Frederick Douglass, who became a leading voice in the fight to abolish slavery, put it more bluntly: "It was a long time before I knew myself to be a *slave*."

But games with other slave children sometimes had an unsettling link to reality. Julia Blanks, who grew up a slave in Texas, remembered

Public Sale.

BY order of the Orphans' Court of Anne Arundel County, the subscriber will expose at Public Sale, on Tuesday, the 4th of October next, all the personal property of Joshua Howard, late of said county, deceased, consisting of

TWELVE NEGROES,

CONSISTING OF

Men, Women, and Children,

HORSES, CATTLE, SHEEP, &

HOGS,

One Wagon

AND

GEARS,

One Yoke of Oxen

AND

CART

with a variety of FARMING UTENSILS HOUSEHOLD AND KITCHEN FURNITURE, Wheat, Rye, and Oats in the Straw; a crop of Tobacco, and a crop of Corn, also a great many other articles too tedious to mention.

Terms of Sale.

All sums of twenty dollars and upwards, six months credit, the purchasers giving note with approved security. All sums under twenty dollars cash.

MARY HOWARD,
Executrix.

September 21.

"Twelve negroes" were offered for sale in this advertisement, along with horses, cattle, oxen, hogs, one wagon, and a cart.

Slave children and the master's children sometimes played together.

that she and her friends made a game of whipping each other with switches. Another game was the auction, in which children imitated the slave market. On one occasion, two slave boys were arguing about how much they were worth, when the master's son wanted to join in. He asked how much he was worth, and the slave boys scornfully answered: "Lord, Marse Frank, you're white. You ain't worth nothing!"

FATHERS AND MOTHERS

Former slaves remembered their parents with great fondness. Nancy Williams's father built extra shelves in their house to store her mother's beautiful quilts. Will Adams's father was a foreman on a large Texas

The auction block was a constant threat to the relationships of people in slave communities.

plantation. Yet, no matter how tired he was at the end of the day, he played with Will every evening. Another slave recalled his father as "a good man" and a "good carpenter [who] could do anything."

Slave mothers were faced with heavier burdens. After long hours at work in the fields or the Big House, they still needed to tend to their own families. Even when pregnant, they were subject to the master's rules. For some women, this meant working until labor set in, delivering a baby, and returning to work the next day. Other new mothers were permitted to stay home after the delivery for anywhere from a few days to a month. Once new mothers were back at work, the job of caring for infants and young children fell mostly to the elderly.

Because of their duties, slave mothers often found it difficult to care for, or sometimes even to see, their children. Frederick Douglass did not remember seeing his mother until he was seven years old. He wrote: "The domestic hearth, with its holy lessons and precious endearments, is abolished in the case of a slave-mother and her children."

COURTSHIP AND ROMANCE

Amid the brutality of plantation life, slaves still found time for romance. One slave recalled how men "would come to the girl they liked, and talk to them at night after the work was done." Another remembered how love blossomed even though the white man was never far away:

> We would just sit and talk with each other. I told him once I didn't love him . . . and then I told him again that I loved him so much I just loved to see him walk. You had to court right there on the place, 'cause they had padderollers.

Many slaveholders respected the courting slaves. Still, falling in love often brought heartache. Some slaves vowed never to marry, for the pain of separation—should a spouse be sold to another plantation—was too much to bear.

Other slaves pledged to marry slaves from different plantations, though masters rarely permitted such unions. In this way, a slave would not have to watch a husband or wife subjected to harsh punishments or cruel treatment. John Anderson summed up the feelings of many: "I did not want to marry a girl from my own place to see her ill-treated." Moses Grandy wrote, "No colored man wishes to live at the house where his wife lives, for he has to endure the continual misery of seeing her . . . abused, without daring to say a word in her defence."

Masters and other white men on the plantation often abused female slaves sexually, frequently fathering their children. James Henry Hammond got at least two of his female slaves pregnant. Mulatto, or mixed race, children were common on Southern plantations. Though they were often the master's children, they were also his slaves.

JUMPING THE BROOM

Though slave marriages were not recognized under U.S. law, slave couples still married and developed unique wedding traditions. One such custom was called "jumping the broomstick."

Most weddings took place on Saturday afternoon or Sunday in the slave quarters. After a procession, the wedding party and guests went to the home of the bride. Bride and groom stood in the center of the room, and someone laid a broomstick across the floor. Another slave, usually an elderly woman, said, "In de eyes of Jesus step into the Holy land of mat-de-money." Arm in arm, the newlyweds stepped or jumped across the broomstick.

No one knows exactly how jumping the broomstick originated, though scholars note that the broom held spiritual significance in some African cultures, marking the beginning of domestic life for a couple. When asked about the tradition, many former slaves simply replied, "Jus' means marryin', dat's all."

On some plantations, the master performed wedding ceremonies and often gave a party for a newly married couple. James Henry Hammond made slave weddings part of the Christmas festivities on his South Carolina plantation. House slaves received extra-special attention. They were married in the Big House, often wearing fancy hand-me-down clothing from the master's family.

One slave remembered that after performing each ceremony, his master would close with the following verse:

> Dat yo' wife
> Dat yo' husban'
> I'se yo marsa
> She yo' missus
> You married.

The slaves knew that their marriage vows were different from those of whites. The absence of the phrase "till death do you part," served as a grim reminder that the master determined the couple's fate. Matthew Jarrett, a former slave from Virginia, described the situation:

> We slaves knowed that them words wasn't bindin'. Don't mean nothin' lessen you say, "What God has jined, caint no man pull asunder. But dey never would say dat. Jus' say, "Now you married."

A wedding dance

Above, *a slave family stood ready to be auctioned off.* **Below,** *a slave mother was pulled away from her child. One of them had probably been sold to another plantation.*

One old black preacher brought the issue into unmistakable clarity, concluding his ceremonies with the words: "Till death or buckra [the white man] part you."

A FAMILIAR HEARTACHE

The worst fear for any slave couple was separation. Most planters made efforts to keep families intact. But when debts mounted, cash was short, or the master died, the slave trader was always there.

If a couple was lucky, they might spend six years together. But some planters had no reservations about breaking up unions that had lasted much longer. In Louisiana, Hosea Bidell was separated from his wife of 25 years. Valentine Miner's wife was sold after 30 years of marriage. After 43 years, Lucy Robinson was torn from her husband.

House slaves were generally more secure than other slaves. Since they were often on intimate terms with the master's family, the master was less willing to part with them. If he did so, it was often as a family.

Unfortunately, field slaves were sold with little regard for their family members. To pay for his daughter's wedding, Ben Johnson's master sold Ben's brother Jim. Slaves often pleaded not to be separated. "Who buys me must buy my son too," shouted one slave from an auction block.

Janie Satterwhite was too young to understand what was happening when she was sold to a new master. As her new owner put her in his carriage, she turned to her parents and said, "Good-bye, I'll be back in de mawnin'."

THE LITTLE SPOTS ALLOWED THEM

All I want in dis creation
Is pretty little wife and big
plantation.

—Slave song

When James Henry Hammond took possession of Silver Bluff plantation in South Carolina on December 8, 1831, he expected to dominate every aspect of his slaves' lives. He would feed them and clothe them. He would decide what tasks they performed and how long they worked.

But Hammond's slaves had other ideas. When they trudged home every evening from the field or the Big House, they entered a very different world—the world of the slave community, about which the white master knew little or nothing.

NEGRO COUNTRY

Many of the first slaves who came to America lived in their master's home or in the lofts of nearby kitchens, sheds, or barns. If the master desired his slaves to have separate cabins, they were often built close to his own dwelling.

Slave quarters

But as the lives of slaves became more restricted, both by law and custom, segregation of the races became more prevalent. By the beginning of the 18th century, the practice of setting aside portions of land, or "quarters," for slaves was widespread. By the mid-18th century, sets of small slave cabins were already visible on the plantation landscape.

Though the cabins varied, they generally were made of wood and consisted of one room. They were often built by the slaves themselves. On Frederick Law Olmsted's first journey to South Carolina in 1852, he described the slave quarters of a local plantation:

Most slave homes were one-room cabins.

> The negro-cabins here, were the smallest I had seen—I thought not more than twelve feet square, inside. They stood in two rows, with a wide street between them. They were built of logs, with no windows—no opening at all, except the doorway, with a chimney of sticks and mud; with no trees about them, no porches, or shades, of any kind.

Some cabins were built of better materials. In Virginia, Olmsted discovered slave homes that offered "various degrees of comfort and commodiousness." The cabins might include glass windows, or at least crude openings cut in the walls to let in air and light. The outside might be whitewashed, and the inside might even have a plank floor. Some slaves, such as those who lived on Sam Aleckson's plantation, were permitted to plant flower gardens outside their homes.

Slaves, with good reason, often complained about their masters' concept of "adequate" housing. John Brown, a former slave from Georgia, protested that "the wind and the rain come in and the smoke will not go out." Robert Shepard, also from Georgia, remembered the cabins having "chimblies made out of stick and red mud. Dem chimblies was all de time catchin' fire."

Some masters permitted only one family to a cabin. Others had several families share quarters. On the South Carolina plantation where Charles Ball had been a slave, 260 slaves shared 38 cabins. Some masters housed and fed their slaves in long, low sheds, which held as many as 30 people each.

Slaves generally had to make the furniture and utensils they needed. Men carved spoons and fashioned plates, bowls, and other kitchen articles out of metal, wood, and dried gourds. Beds might be boards covered with straw or mattresses of corn shucks, though some slaves built more substantial cots. Others merely slept on the ground.

Masters distributed some household goods, such as thin cotton blankets that were expected to last two to three years. Slave women sewed warm and beautiful quilts. Sometimes plantation mistresses organized quilting parties, as did slave women themselves.

Inside, slave homes were simple. Most furnishings were homemade.

Sleeping arrangements were serious matters, determined by African folk customs. Often slaves slept with blankets pulled over their heads, even if their feet froze, to ward off evil spirits that might be lurking in the dark. Beds were positioned east to west, as was the tradition in parts of Africa, so one would not sleep in "the crossways of the world."

"WHO IS THAT YONDER ALL DRESSED IN RED?"

Most slaveholders spent between 7 and 10 dollars a year to clothe each adult slave. Some bought ready-made clothing. To save money, others bought materials that slave women could use to make clothing for their own families, and often for the master's family. In 1854, Robert Collins, a planter from Macon, Georgia, wrote:

> The proper and usual quantity of clothes for plantation hands is two suits of cotton for spring and summer, and two suits of woolen for winter; four pair of shoes and three hats . . . make up the year's allowance.

Many planters also contributed socks and underclothes. But even the most generous clothing allotments did not make it possible for slaves to change clothes more than once a week.

Many slaves found their coarse, heavy cotton shirts to be durable, but uncomfortable. One slave from Virginia protested that the fabric "was jus' like needles when it was new. Never did have to scratch our back. Jus' wriggle yo' shoulders and yo' back was scratched." Many a small boy found himself grateful for older brothers who had broken in their rough shirts before handing them down.

Shoes weren't much better. The crude measurements and rough materials of the period—usually cardboard and sheepskin—added up to painful and swollen feet. During spring and summer, many slaves worked barefoot. Mary Reynolds remembered praying for "the end of tribulation and the end of beatings and for shoes that fit our feet."

Red was the preferred color for clothing among slave men and women. For many Africans, red was not only a regal but also a religious color. Among many tribes, red symbolized blood, regarded as sacred. For women, red meant life and fertility; for men, it stood for war and the hunt.

From time to time, masters and mistresses bought or made red articles for their favorite slaves. But the slaves learned not to depend on the occasional handout. Instead, they used dyes to color their clothing—tan, gray, or red, depending on whether they needed the item for work, church, or special occasions.

"DE BES' COOK IN DE COUNTRY"

Masters tended to distribute food during the weekend, in time for special Sunday dinners. Weekly rations generally consisted of eight quarts of cornmeal and two and a half to four pounds of pork or bacon per person. Some masters handed out small amounts of sugar, coffee, molasses, and whiskey.

Slaves supplemented their diets in numerous ways. A successful hunting expedition might bring home squirrels, rabbits, groundhogs,

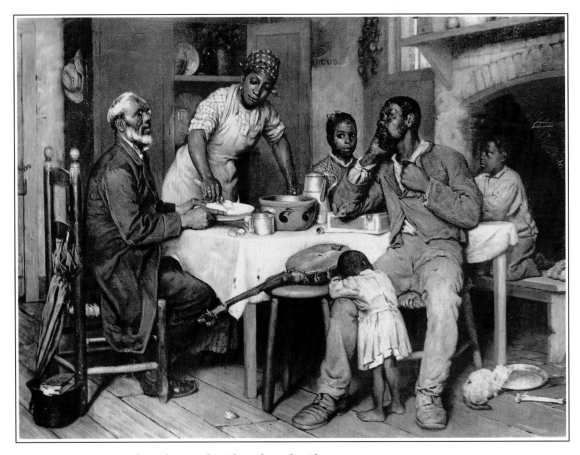

A pastor shared a meal with a slave family.

or possums. (Squirrel pie served with dumplings was considered a delicacy.) Trout, mussels, crabs, and catfish came from nearby streams and rivers. Some slaves raised chickens for cooking. Those who were allowed to have small gardens added sweet potatoes, beans, cabbage, squash, and okra to their diets.

Some masters skimped on rations to cut expenses or to deliberately keep slaves weak. If so, slaves might resort to stealing. "The very best remedy for hog-stealing," advised one Virginia planter, "is to give . . . plenty of pork to eat."

Food was cooked in large fireplaces, at least four feet wide or larger, where several tasks could be performed at once. As one slave recalled:

> 'Taters and cornpone was roasted in de ashes and most of de other victuals was biled [boiled] in de big old pots what swing on cranes over de coals. Dey had long-handled fryin pans and heavy iron skillets ... and ovens of all sizes to bake in. ... Dere never was no better tastin' somepin t'eat dan dat cooked in dem old cook-things in open fireplaces.

Slave cooks combined cuisines from many cultures to develop a distinctive style of their own. Dishes such as coosh-coosh and ash-cake were variations of recipes passed down from West Africa. The use of spicy peppers, oils, and vinegars came from African and Caribbean traditions. Many slaves believed that sesame seeds, also from Africa, brought good luck. Slave cooks baked the seeds into everything from breads and rolls to cookies.

"SICKNESS IN MUH TIME"

It was in the master's interest to maintain the health of his slaves. But during the 18th and 19th centuries, poor diets, bad hygiene, and primitive medical care made for short lives among both whites and blacks.

According to folk wisdom, blacks were less vulnerable than whites to certain diseases, such as malaria and yellow fever. While this was generally true, slaves were vulnerable to many other kinds of disease. Henry Baker recalled:

> Dere wuz much ... sickness 'mong dem. ... De diseases we had wuz de measles, colic, penumony, [pneumonia]. ... I'membah once we got down wid penumony. Der wuz six uv uz in bed at one time. We got er white doctor to come see us but de main remedy we had wuz tuh go tuh de woods en git pine tops tuh boil en sweat ourself wid hit.

Infectious diseases such as measles, smallpox, cholera, and scrofula—a form of tuberculosis—often devastated slave communities. Living in close and unsanitary quarters, slaves were prime targets for disease.

When slaves became ill, the master or mistress usually treated them, though in cases of serious illness, slaveholders summoned a doctor. Many slaves, suspicious of white medical practices, either concealed their illnesses or turned to "root doctors" within the slave community. Root doctors relied on various herbs to treat any number of aches and pains. Such treatments had been used in Africa and the Caribbean and often combined medicine and magic.

It was common for the master himself to turn to such folk remedies. Said one, "It is seldom that I call in a physician. We Doctor upon [use the services of] an old woman slave and have first rate luck." Upon

A funeral procession

seeing the successful results of a folk remedy, another wrote, "These simple remedies resorted to by [slaves] are generally approved by experience and sometimes condescendingly adopted by science."

"HARK FROM THE TOMB"

When a slave died, funeral preparations began almost immediately. The deceased was never left unattended. Relatives and friends would "set" with the family, often singing and chanting over the body. Usually, a personal article of the deceased, a hat, a shirt, or a dress, was hung from the family's door—an announcement to all that a death had occurred. The body was washed and wrapped in clean white cloth. Then it was laid on a "coolin' board," which resembled an ironing board, until placed in a coffin.

Slave funerals were often held at night so that people from neighboring plantations could attend. Funerals were at once solemn ceremonies, pageants, and community efforts. At the grave site, mourners sang, chanted, and shouted. The body was buried with its head to the west—so the deceased would not have to turn around when the angel Gabriel sounded his trumpet in the east.

Some burial rituals were extensions of West African traditions, meant to prevent ghosts from bothering the living or to aid the deceased on a safe spiritual journey. One slave who had been a priest of his tribe buried his young son with a canoe, a paddle, and bow and arrows—to ensure that his son's soul would travel safely back to Africa.

LET YOUR MOTTO BE RESISTANCE

Brethren, arise, arise! Strike for your lives and liberties. Now is the day and the hour. . . .
Rather die free men than live to be slaves. . . . Let your motto be resistance! resistance!
RESISTANCE!
　　　　—Henry Highland Garnet,
　　African-American abolitionist

D e rabbit is de slickest o' all de animals de Lawd ever made. He ain't de biggest, an' he ain't de loudest but he sho am de slickest." So spoke Brer Rabbit, one of many characters found in slave folktales.

Few slaves could read or write. So slaves relied on other types of expression. African folktales, passed down orally, taught slaves valuable lessons about survival. At the center of many stories was the "animal trickster," a small, smart creature such as Brer Rabbit or Anansi the Spider. Like the slaves, the trickster had to rely on his wits to escape danger. Powerful, cruel, and slow-witted animals in the stories represented the master and his family.

Brer Rabbit taught slaves that "you hafto use yo' haid fo mo'on a hat rack." If the strong could dominate the weak, the tales showed again and again that the smart could dominate the strong. One former slave said folktales taught him "more in my early childhood about how to live than I have learned since."

Slaves also used songs to communicate and to make subtle fun of their masters. Harriet Jacobs recorded that blacks ridiculed stingy whites by singing:

> Poor Massa, so dey say
> Down in de heel, so dey say
> Got no money, so dey say
> Not one shillin', so dey say
> God A'mighty bress you, so dey say

"Once in a while among a mass of nonsense and wild frolic," Frederick Douglass recalled, "a sharp hit was given to the meanness of the slaveholders." Another song mocked:

> We raise de wheat
> Dey gib us de corn
> We bake de bread
> Dey gib us de crust
> We sif [sift] the meal
> Dey gib us de huss [husk]
> We peel de meat
> Dey gib us de skin
> And dat's de way
> Dey take us in

"TO TALK WITH OUR HEARTS"

Slaves had brought powerful religious traditions with them from Africa. Yet masters imposed their own religion, Christianity, on the slaves. Masters, mistresses, and local ministers read to slaves from the

Bible. Sometimes white missionaries visited slave quarters, bringing religious instruction.

A favorite text of the masters was from St. Paul's Letter to the Ephesians, which instructed slaves to "be obedient to those who are your earthly masters, with fear and trembling, in singleness of heart, as to Christ." One minister addressed his slave congregation:

> Poor creatures . . . what faults you are guilty of towards your masters and mistresses are faults against God himself . . . your masters and mistresses are God's overseers, and that if you are faulty towards them, God himself will punish you severely for it in the next world, unless you repent.

"Be nice to massa and missus," West Turner, a former slave from Virginia, recalled being instructed. "Don't be mean, be obedient, and work hard. That was all the Sunday school lesson they taught us." Nancy Williams was more critical of the white church. "That ol' white preachin' wasn't nothin. . . . " she said. "Ol white precher used to talk with their tongues without saying nothin', but Jesus told us slaves to talk with our hearts."

Self-taught black preachers often spoke of "Jubilee"— the promise of delivery from bondage.

To make Christianity suitable to their own needs, slaves focused on a religion that promised "Jubilee"—the deliverance from bondage. Instead of stern lectures on obeying authority, self-taught black preachers told of Moses leading the Jews out of slavery. "We wanted to sing, pray, and serve God in our way," explained Cornelius Garner.

Religious songs called spirituals helped slaves feel connected to each other and to God. The songs identified slaves as "de people dat is born of God," who were bound to go to heaven. Worship services were filled with singing, shouting, clapping hands, and joyful screams. One slave explained: "[Religion] needs a little motion—specially if you gwine feel de spirret."

Masters sometimes forbade such worship services, fearing that slaves might use the gatherings to organize revolts. So meetings were often held in secret. After breaking up one such "invisible" church service near the plantation where West Turner worked, patrollers beat and whipped the slaves. Turner remembered one patroller saying, "If I catch you here servin' God, I'll beat you. You ain't got no time to serve God. We bought you to serve us."

To keep their meetings secret, slaves devised special codes. On one plantation, whenever slaves began singing "Steal Away to Jesus," others knew that a religious meeting was scheduled for that evening.

"IF I HAD BEEN ABLE TO READ AND WRITE"

Reading and writing were also forbidden for slaves. For planters, literate slaves meant slaves who could forge passes and read newspapers, the Bible, and other documents—without the master's censorship.

Most of all, planters feared that literacy could lead to revolt. For once a slave learned to read and write, as Josiah Henson did, he or she would "feel more deeply and bitterly the oppression under which I had toiled and groaned . . . [and] do something for the rescue and elevation of those who were suffering the same evils I had endured."

Whitemarsh Seabrook, a planter from South Carolina, declared that anyone who wished slaves to learn to read and write belonged in a lunatic asylum. "Our white folks didn't believe in niggers larning' anything," slave Sarah Wilson remarked. "Dey thought hit would make de niggers harder to keep slaves, an' to make dem wuk."

Yet slaves who could read and write were everywhere. On almost every plantation at least one slave was literate. Educated men and women were valuable members of the slave community. Not only could they pass on news of the outside world to their fellow slaves but they could also teach their skills to others.

Despite laws forbidding slaves to read and write, many masters and mistresses undertook to instruct them. In some cases, masters and mistresses singled out house servants, or a favorite slave who persisted in asking to be taught. John Bates's mistress tried to teach him to read and write, but he complained that his "head jes' too thick." James Singleton's father, on the other hand, received a "stolen ejucation," courtesy of the master's wife.

The whites' reasons for teaching their slaves varied. For Protestants who believed that everyone should be able to read the Bible, the lessons were a matter of duty and conscience. One young master considered slave literacy a matter of practical convenience: "The law could go to hell since he simply had to have someone literate among the slaves."

Slaves usually made the most of the opportunities given to them. Elijah P. Marrs remembered an old slave who taught others to read late at night. Slave children sometimes sat outside white schoolhouses, memorizing the lessons they overheard. Mandy Jones remembered:

> De white chillun thought a heap of cullud chillun, an'
> when dey come out o' school wid deir books in deir han's,
> dey take de cullud chillun, an' slip off somewhere, an'
> learns de culled chillun deir lessons.

Other slaves would meet at night in a clearing and study by the light of pinewood torches.

Where masters disapproved, slaves caught reading and writing were subjected to harsh punishments. One slave, Tom Hawkins, recalled

Frederick Douglass, who escaped slavery and became an educated man, was a leading advocate for the abolition of slavery.

how his master, Dr. Cannon, cut off the thumbs of a carriage driver who had learned to read and write. Hal Hutson was whipped. Margrett Nickerson, when a young girl, helped dig out an older slave, "Uncle George Bull," who had been beaten and buried for knowing how to read and write.

"STANDING UP TO THE MAN"

In a variety of ways, slaves expressed their dissatisfaction daily. Their acts of "silent sabotage" did not usually threaten the welfare of the master and his family. But they did cause considerable aggravation.

"Revenge against work" was revenge against the master's power and his wallet. On any given day, slaves might slow the pace of work. They dragged their feet, "misunderstood" orders, broke tools, maimed work animals, and pretended to be sick. In extreme cases, slaves even hurt themselves to avoid work.

Since the master already thought his slaves simple-minded, slaves sometimes played along. The more ignorant they seemed, the less work they had to do. "They can neither hoe, nor ditch, chop wood, nor perform any kind of labor with a white man's skill," wrote an exasperated Daniel Dennett, editor of the Louisiana *Planter's Banner*. A mechanic in Savannah wrote in his journal, "I happened to be swearing at a negro who was helping me or rather hindering me."

Masters complained about the slaves' apparent inability to use tools or perform routine tasks, even after they had been shown repeatedly how to do so. Almost daily, overseers and masters confronted slaves who "disremembered" their instructions. Frances Butler Leigh captured the frustration of planters in her diary:

> I generally found that if I wanted a thing done first I had to tell the negroes to do it, then show them how, and finally do it myself. Their way of managing not to do it was very ingenious, for they were always perfectly good-tempered, and received my orders with, "Dat's so missus; just as missus says," and then somehow or other left the thing undone.

In an essay describing diseases "peculiar to the Negro," a Louisiana physician identified an ailment that he called Dyaesthesia Aethiopica ("irresponsibility of the Ethiopian"):

> The individuals affected with this complaint . . . are apt to do much mischief, which appears as if intentional. . . . Thus they break, waste, and destroy everything they handle, abuse horses and cattle, tear, burn, or rend their clothing. . . . They slight their work. . . . They raise disturbances with their overseers. . . . The overseers call it "rascality" supposing that the mischief is intentionally done.

Stealing was another act of defiance, with the theft of food and drink the most common offense. But outsmarting the master, as did the small and clever creatures in folktales, was often just as important to slaves as the articles they stole.

Arson was a more destructive form of rebellion. Many a master dreaded the thought of his plantation buildings, or even the entire crop, going up in flames. Arson was hard to detect, and thus easy for slaves to accomplish. As a result, fire insurance companies were often reluctant to write policies for slaveholders.

Most slaveholders insisted that they did not fear their slaves and, in fact, relied on them for protection. Even amid rumors of slave rebellion, slaveholders believed that other planters' slaves were at fault—never their own.

But every so often, news that a slave had killed his master or mistress would send shock waves through the white community. Thad White, a Virginia slaveholder, explained that "there were just enough instances of masters who had been killed by a slave to [justify] . . . the whites' . . . sense of insecurity."

Slaveholders and their families were especially fearful of being poisoned. Many slaves brought from Africa knowledge of deadly plants and poisons, which, when necessary, they put to use. Accounts of masters and mistresses being poisoned by arsenic, ground glass, or "spiders beaten up in buttermilk" increased the fear in white households.

Slaves sometimes had no recourse but to strike out. Solomon Northup almost killed his owner for attacking him with an ax. One housemaid told her mistress that if she did not quit calling her names, she would "take an iron and split her brains out."

"TO RISE AND BURN AND KILL US ALL"

During the night of August 22, 1791, a wall of fire rose on the French colony of Saint-Domingue (now Haiti) in the Caribbean. The blaze swept across the northern plain and spread in all directions, moving at once toward the mountains and the sea.

Enormous gusts of wind drove the flames on: through forests and fields thick with cotton, sugarcane, and coffee; to warehouses, sugar mills, and plantation homes. The slaves had arisen in rebellion. The leader of the uprising, Toussaint-Louverture, pointed his musket toward the fire and told his followers: "There is your liberty."

Toussaint-Louverture led a violent rebellion in 1791.

As word of the slave uprising spread, Toussaint's words echoed in the ears of slaves throughout the South. His deeds inspired slaves to dream of freedom, but gave nightmares to masters.

One Virginia planter wrote, "These insurrections have alarmed my wife so as really to endanger her health, and I have not slept without anxiety in three months. Our nights are spent in listening to noises." Some planters slept with pistols under their pillows. Others readied their most important possessions in tote bags, prepared to flee at a moment's notice. In Alabama, some planters built pens in the woods that would serve as hiding places from rebelling slaves. Mary Chestnut, the wife of a prominent South Carolina planter, wrote: "How long will they resist the seductive and irresistible call: 'Rise, kill, and be free'?"

Southern slaves lived scattered on distant plantations. They could not easily coordinate a mass rebellion. Unlike the islands of the Caribbean, the American South had no interior mountain ranges into which slaves could escape and establish independent communities. Some runaway slaves did hide out in the Dismal Swamp along the border of Virginia and North Carolina. But they could not survive there for long.

Nevertheless, the oldest and most stable slaveholding states of the South—Virginia and South Carolina—witnessed three significant slave rebellions in the early 19th century. The rebellions stunned planters. If the slaves could strike for freedom there, they might do so anywhere.

The leaders of the rebellions shared a common bond. Each was a member of the "privileged class" of slaves. Gabriel Prosser was a blacksmith. Nat Turner was a foreman and preacher. Denmark Vesey was a sailor who had bought his freedom. Each had also learned to read and write.

A REVOLT, A CONSPIRACY, A REBELLION

In the summer of 1800, Gabriel Prosser organized some one thousand slaves in Henrico County, Virginia. Armed with clubs, knives, and guns, Prosser and his small army planned to march to Richmond, the state capital. An eyewitness to the conspiracy, a slave named Ben, later testified in court about Prosser's plan:

> They were to kill Mr. Prosser [Gabriel's master], Mr. Mosby, and all the neighbors, and then proceed to Richmond, where they would kill everybody, take the treasury, and divide the money amongst the soldiers; after which he would fortify Richmond. . . . If the white people agreed to their freedom they would then hoist a white flag, and he would dine and drink with the merchants of the city.

But Prosser and his men never made it to Richmond. Rains flooded the main roads and slowed the conspirators down. Meanwhile, in Richmond, local authorities had been alerted to Prosser's plan by two slaves. Led by Governor James Monroe, the local militia met the slaves. No battle took place, but Prosser and 30 of his followers were arrested, tried, and hanged.

In 1822 Denmark Vesey, who as a sailor had traveled to Haiti, organized a plot to seize the city of Charleston and hold it in exchange for the abolition of slavery in South Carolina. "He replied we are free," said one of Vesey's coconspirators, "but the white people here won't let us be so."

Meeting at Vesey's house, Vesey and his followers "determined to have arms . . . and each man put in 12½ cents towards that purpose." In time, they built up a large store of weapons, which included daggers and bayonets. Vesey also hoped to raid the city's two arsenals for guns and ammunition.

The rebellion was set to take place during the weekend of July 14, when many whites would be away from the city to escape the summer heat. But on the evening before the revolt, a slave turned informant and warned authorities of the plan. Like Prosser, Vesey and 35 of his followers were tried and hanged.

No slave uprising in the United States equaled the impact of Nat Turner's rebellion in 1831. Turner, known among his fellow slaves as "The Prophet," believed that God had chosen him to lead his people out of bondage.

On a hot August evening in 1831, Turner and eight followers embarked on what they regarded as a holy crusade through Southampton County, Virginia. Forty-eight hours later, the group—by then numbering close to 70—had slaughtered nearly 60 whites, including Turner's master and his family. Turner later recalled at his trial:

> As it was my object to carry terror and devastation wherever we went, I placed fifteen to twenty of the best armed and most to be relied on in front, who generally approached the houses as fast as their horses could run. This was for two purposes—to prevent their escape and strike terror into the inhabitants.

Some three thousand armed men came to Southampton to hunt Turner. He managed to elude capture for almost two months. When

Nat Turner was apprehended and later hanged for a revolt that left 60 whites dead.

finally caught, he was tried and hanged. At his trial, Turner refused to plead guilty, stating that he did not feel guilty.

Slaveholders never forgot Nat Turner, as they would never forget Toussaint-Louverture, Gabriel Prosser, or Denmark Vesey. Although no major slave uprising occurred in the United States after Turner's rebellion, slaveholders remained uneasy. George Washington's niece described the atmosphere as "a smothered volcano—we know not when, or where . . . but we know that death in the most horrid form threatens us." As a result of the "Southampton affair," more stringent slave codes were passed, and many states strengthened their militias and slave patrols.

RUNAWAYS AND THE "PADDYROLLERS"

Short of rebellion, the most aggressive form of resistance for a slave was running away. Who took this risky gamble? Runaways were generally single men between the ages of 16 and 35. One third of runaways were skilled laborers and house slaves. Fewer women attempted to run, largely because of family obligations and a lack of survival skills.

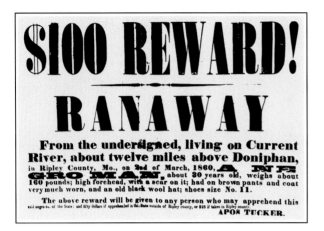

A white owner sought to reclaim a runaway slave, called only "A Negro Man" in this advertisement.

Most slaves ran away to escape work, avoid punishment, protest a change in their routine, or calm their anger. One former slave noted that slaves ran away "to keep from doing something," namely fighting, or perhaps killing, the overseer or master. Others ran to join loved ones who had been sold to another planter. Advertisements for runaways mentioned that a slave was "no doubt trying to reach his wife" or was "searching for daughter and infant son."

James Henry Hammond found that if he could not prevent slaves from running away, he could at least try to lure them back before they were caught by patrollers. To encourage runaways to surrender voluntarily, Hammond announced a policy of reduced punishment. He threatened 10 lashes for each day absent for those who had to be captured, but only 3 per day for those who returned on their own.

RUNNING TO FREEDOM

But many slaves never returned. Each year, hundreds successfully escaped to Canada, Mexico, and the Northern United States—places where slavery was not practiced.

The Northern states were rapidly becoming industrialized. Northern industry drew its labor force not from slaves but from European immigrants, arriving in greater numbers every year. Over time, many

This slave mother killed two of her children when she was caught trying to escape with them. "Rather dead, than slave," she said.

Northerners became increasingly critical of the South's "peculiar institution" of slavery.

Abolitionist, or antislavery, societies were formed in the North as early as 1775. By the early 19th century, most Northern states had outlawed slavery. Runaways who managed to reach these states were usually allowed to live free.

THE UNDERGROUND RAILROAD

"By to-morrow evening's mail, you will receive two volumes of 'The Irrepressible Conflict' bound in black. After perusal please forward and oblige." So read the message. In reality, the recipient was not getting two books, but two of the many runaway slaves "riding" the Underground Railroad.

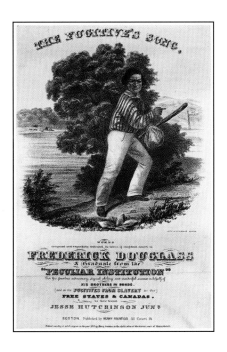

The cover page of a song, published in 1845, called "The Fugitive's Song" and dedicated to Frederick Douglass, "a graduate from the 'Peculiar Institution' "

Conceived sometime in 1804, the Underground Railroad was an intricate system of escape routes leading from the South into the North, Midwest, and Canada. "Stations" were places of shelter. "Agents" were those men and women who helped the runaways. "Conductors" were supervisors who handled travel arangements. One of the most famous conductors on the Underground Railroad was Harriet Tubman, herself an escaped slave, said to have helped free more than 300 others.

Despite the aid, runaway slaves faced an arduous and dangerous journey. Traveling from Missouri to Iowa, Adeline Henderson remembered, "We had to ride all night in wagons from one station to the other and hide in the woods and old houses during the day." Allen Sidney and his family, on their escape to Canada, rode underneath a wagonload of hay, traveling at night and resting in barns.

For many Americans, just helping runaway slaves was not enough. A growing number of Northerners wanted to prevent the spread of slavery into new states or to abolish slavery altogether. But Southerners, with an agricultural economy heavily dependent on slaves, were not about to give up their chief source of labor. By the mid-1850s, hostilities were brewing between North and South. The United States was on the verge of civil war.

"We shall stay here and watch the current of events," wrote Frederick Douglass in early 1861. He did not have to wait long. In April, shots at Fort Sumter, South Carolina, thundered throughout the land. The "Jubilee War" was at hand.

Harriet Tubman helped hundreds of slaves escape through the Underground Railroad.

CHILDREN OF PROMISE

When will Jehovah hear our cry,
And free the sons of Africa?
                        —Slave spiritual

Now everything wuz stirred up for a long spell, fo' de war to free us come on," Temple Wilson said, recalling the start of the Civil War in April 1861. For many slaves, the opening guns of the war—the firing on Fort Sumter—signaled the beginning of the end for the South's "peculiar institution." Already their joy could be heard in many places throughout the South:

> No more auction block for me
> No more, No more
> No more auction block for me
> Many thousand gone
> No more driver's lash for me
> No more, No more
> No more driver's lash for me
> Many thousand gone

"Contrabands" fled to this Union camp during the Civil War.

While some slaves were unaware of the terrible conflict between North and South, others waited anxiously for news of the war. J. W. King remembered that at his plantation, slaves "would slip up to a open winder at de big house . . . and listen to what was read f'om a letter. De next day, dat's what folks would talk about in de fields."

Slaves who lived near the North-South border did more than listen. As Union (Northern) troops approached, thousands of slaves fled their plantations and flooded into military camps. Calling the runaways "contraband" (property seized from the enemy), the Union army protected them. Historians estimate that 500,000 slaves claimed their freedom in this way.

Freed slaves helped the Union war effort in countless ways. Some, such as Susie King Taylor, worked as cooks, nurses, and laundresses for the troops. Others served as carpenters, laborers, and drovers. Some acted as spies, slipping back and forth across enemy lines to gather information. In 1862 the Reverend Charles Colcock Jones Sr.

expressed his concern about slaves' espionage in a letter to his eldest son, Charles Jr.:

> They are traitors who may pilot an enemy into your *bed-chamber!* They know every road and swamp and creek and plantation in the county, and are the worst spies.

Among the more clever methods in intelligence gathering were those of a black couple in Fredericksburg, Virginia. Through the creative use of laundry and clothesline, they signaled Confederate (Southern) troop movements to Union commanders. The husband, Dabney, took a Union officer to a clearing that overlooked the Rappahannock River. He pointed to the enemy lines:

> You see my wife over there; she washes for the [Confederate] officers . . . and as soon as she hears about any movement or anything going on, she comes down and moves the clothes on that line so I can understand it in a minute. That there gray shirt is Longstreet; and when she takes it off, it means he's gone down about Richmond. That white shirt means Hill; and when she moves it up to the west end of the line, Hill's corps has moved up stream. That red one is Stonewall. He's down on the right now, and if he moves, she will move that red shirt.

MARCHING TOWARD FREEDOM

Many African Americans wanted to fight—to share in the promised "Fires of Jubilee," preached to them so often. Yet the Union at first refused to enlist blacks, largely because of prejudice and the belief that African Americans, especially slaves, were incapable of good soldiering. In an angry 1861 editorial, "Fighting Rebels with Only One Hand," Frederick Douglass thundered:

> What upon earth is the matter with the American government and people? . . . Why does the government reject the negro? Is he not a man? . . . Men in earnest don't fight with one hand, when they might fight with two . . . a man drowning would not refuse to be saved even by a colored hand.

Finally, in the fall of 1862, President Abraham Lincoln authorized the enlistment of black regiments. On November 7, 1862, the First South Carolina Volunteers formed, led by Colonel Thomas Wentworth Higginson, a noted Massachusetts abolitionist. The regiment participated in a number of successful raids throughout South Carolina and Georgia. Higginson was impressed by the black soldiers' courage and fighting skills. He noted in his diary, later published as *Army Life in a Black Regiment,* "that the key to successful prosecution of this war lies in the . . . employment of black troops."

By 1863, the Union army had 58 African-American regiments, totaling more than 37,000 troops. Some 10,000 more African Americans enlisted in the navy. The most famous black regiment was the 54th Massachusetts, formed in February 1863. Colonel Robert Gould Shaw, son of a leading abolitionist family in Boston, was chosen to

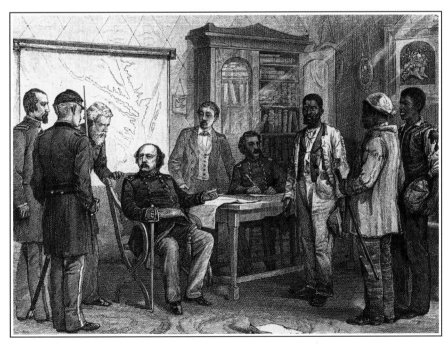

Escaped slave men turned themselves in to Union army officers.

Above, *thousands of slaves fought for the Union during the Civil War.* Below, *an ad urged free black men to join contraband soldiers in the Union cause.*

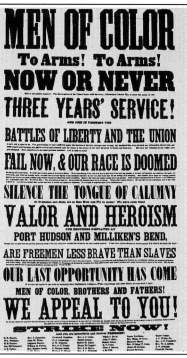

train and command the unit. The 54th contained 600 free blacks and slaves, including 2 of Frederick Douglass's sons.

After training in Boston, Shaw's troops were chosen to lead an assault on Fort Wagner, near Charleston, South Carolina. On July 18, 1863, the 54th attacked, only to be beaten back by Confederate troops. Almost half the regiment, including 26-year-old Shaw, lost their lives in the battle.

Yet the bravery and spirit of Shaw's "good soldiers" gave a triumphant response to those who doubted the ability of African Americans to fight. As one correspondent for the *New York Tribune* wrote, the battle made "Fort Wagner such a name to the colored race as Bunker Hill has been . . . to the . . . Yankees."

The most notorious episode of the war involving black soldiers was the April 1864 Fort Pillow Massacre, in which Confederate troops slaughtered black soldiers rather than accept their surrender. Eli Carlton, a black private, testified before a congressional committee that he "saw 23 men shot after they surrendered; I made 24." The cry "Remember Fort Pillow!" spurred more black enlistments.

BEHIND THE LINES

In the Deep South, far from the advancing Union troops, most slaves were expected to carry out their usual duties on the plantation. But instead of working only for their masters, slaves also contributed to the Confederate war effort.

Their tasks included growing and harvesting food and working in Southern factories and railroads. Some slaves aided Confederate troops. They dug fortifications and trenches, carried water at battlefields and camps, tended the wounded, and buried the dead. A body servant might carry his master's possessions into camp, hold his horse, shine his boots, nurse his wounds, and bring his body home if he were killed.

Some slaves even chose to fight for the Confederacy. In 1865, Jefferson Davis, president of the Confederate States of America, signed

These slaves were fleeing the approach of the Confederate army under General Stonewall Jackson.

the Negro Soldier Act, allowing slaves—with their masters' permission—to enlist in the Confederate army. Two companies of black soldiers were mustered. But before they saw any action, the Confederacy surrendered.

"SIXTY-THREE IS THE JUBILEE"

On September 22, 1862, President Lincoln called a meeting at the White House. He informed his cabinet that he intended to issue a Proclamation of Emancipation, whereby slaves living in states still in rebellion would be declared free as of January 1, 1863.

African Americans in both the North and South rejoiced. Charlotte S. Forten, a black woman living and teaching on the Sea Islands off the coast of South Carolina, noted in her diary that January 1 was "the most glorious day this nation has yet seen." William C.

Nell, presiding officer of the African-American Union Progressive Association, declared: "New Year's Day . . . by this proclamation is henceforth invested with new significance and imperishable glory."

To many blacks, the coming of the Union soldiers, the defeat of the Confederacy, and the end of slavery were nothing short of God's handiwork. Seldom had their prayers been answered so precisely as when Union soldiers marched onto their plantations, entered the Big House, and ordered their master to free them. A former South Carolina slave recalled: "Us looked for the Yankees [Union troops] . . . like us look for de Savior and de host of angels at the second comin'."

In eastern Virginia, within earshot of the battle raging at Manassas, an elderly slave prepared Sunday dinner for her white family, faithfully performing her duty as she had done for many years. But she greeted each cannon volley that the Yankees delivered with a subdued exclamation: "Ride on, Massa Jesus!"

"THE DOOR IS BROKE DOWN"

No single attitude marked blacks' response to freedom. The feelings ran from fear to confusion, sadness to jubilation, pity to respect to hatred for their former masters. Many slaves believed that the will of God had at last been realized. Said one Nashville preacher:

A Union soldier reading the Emancipation Proclamation to a slave family

We was all like the children of Israel in Egypt, a cryin' and cryin' and a groanin' and groanin', and no Moses came with the Lord's word to order the door broke down, that we might walk through and be free. Now the big, ugly door is broke down, bless the Lord. . . . Didn't I tell you to pray and not to faint away. . . . He who opened the sea would deliver us sure, and not thanks to the taskmasters, who would never let us go if they could have held on to us? But they couldn't—no they couldn't do that, 'cause the Lord he was with us.

New possibilities suddenly presented themselves. Margaret Hughes, a young slave in South Carolina, heard that the Union soldiers were coming. She ran to her aunt for comfort but found the old woman in the best of spirits. "Child," Margaret's aunt reassured her, "we going to have such a good time a settin' at de white folks' table, a eating off de white folks' table, and a rocking in de big rocking chair."

As Union troops captured Confederate cities, many slaves rejoiced.

Even as slaves reveled in freedom, most showed remarkable discipline and restraint. Many waited for the master or mistress to confirm their freedom, rather than assert it independently. Few slaves made an attempt to humiliate or antagonize their former masters. One who had enlisted in the Union army, for example, came back to his old home to see his former mistress. She reminded him that she had once cared for him when he was sick, "and now you are fighting me!" The slave replied, "No'm, I ain't fighting you. I'm fighting to get free."

Despite emancipation, blacks realized that they were not like other Americans. George G. King, who had endured an especially harsh enslavement on a South Carolina plantation, knew this difference only too well from experience. "The Master said we were all free," King recalled, "but that don't mean we was white. And it don't mean we is equal."

HOW FREE IS FREE?

In 1865, the Thirteenth Amendment to the United States Constitution abolished slavery, formally freeing all slaves in the United States. One Virginia freedman compared the newly freed slaves to "a bird let out of a cage. . . . when the door is opened . . . [the bird] makes a curious fluttering for awhile. It was just so with the [slaves]. They didn't know at first what to do with themselves. But got sobered pretty soon."

Indeed, soon after emancipation, African Americans faced harsh realities. Despite the passage of the Fourteenth and Fifteenth Amendments—which extended citizenship and civil rights to blacks and granted black men the right to vote—freedom offered no easy solutions. Instead it often brought new confrontations with racism, discrimination, and violence. Many former slaves found that their greatest challenge was simply living safely and freely, especially in the South.

After the war, secret societies such as the Knights of White Camellia and the Ku Klux Klan used violence and terror to intimidate African Americans. By the 1880s, state legislatures thoughout the South had passed "Jim Crow laws" or "Black Codes." These laws denied blacks access to everything from public bathrooms to public schools, drinking

*A newly emancipated family, in a photograph taken soon after
the Civil War*

An old photograph bears a hasty scribble dating it 1863. "Isaac and Rosa," reads the caption. "Emancipated Slave Children, from the Free Schools of Louisiana." Children such as Isaac and Rosa faced a future of uncertainty and struggle, as the United States began a long journey toward independence, equality, and dignity for all.

fountains to restaurants, waiting rooms to streetcars, hotels to hospitals. The laws also stripped blacks of their civil and political rights. In many ways, the laws were slavery in everything but name.

Though emancipated, Harriet Jacobs still longed for real freedom and security. "The dream of my life is not yet realized," she said. "I do not sit with my children in a home of my own. I still long for a hearthstone . . . however humble." Like countless other blacks, Jacobs knew that emancipation was only a beginning. The African Americans' struggle for independence, equality, and dignity would continue, for days, and years, and generations to come.

SELECTED BIBLIOGRAPHY

Allison, Robert J., ed. *The Interesting Narrative of the Life of Olaudah Equiano, Written by Himself.* New York: Bedford Books, 1995.

Andrews, William L., and McFeely, William S., eds. *Narrative of the Life of Frederick Douglass, an American Slave, Written by Himself.* New York: W. W. Norton, 1997.

Aptheker, Herbert. *American Negro Slave Revolts.* New York: Columbia University Press, 1943.

Blassingame, John W. *The Slave Community: Plantation Life in the Antebellum South.* New York: Oxford University Press, 1979.

_____. *Slave Testimony: Two Centuries of Letters, Speeches, Interviews, and Autobiographies.* Baton Rouge: Louisiana State University Press, 1977.

Escott, Paul D. *Slavery Remembered: A Record of Twentieth Century Slave Narratives.* Chapel Hill: University of North Carolina Press, 1979.

Fox-Genovese, Elizabeth. *Within the Plantation Household: Black and White Women of the Old South.* Chapel Hill: University of North Carolina Press, 1988.

Genovese, Eugene. *Roll, Jordan, Roll: The World the Slaves Made.* New York: Alfred A. Knopf, 1972.

_____. *From Rebellion to Revolution.* Baton Rouge: Louisiana State University Press, 1979.

Gutman, Herbert. *The Black Family in Slavery and Freedom, 1750– 1925.* New York: Random House, 1976.

Harding, Vincent. *There Is a River.* New York: Harcourt Brace, 1981.

Hurmence, Belinda, ed. *My Folks Don't Want Me to Talk about Slavery.* Winston-Salem, North Carolina: John F. Blair, 1984.

Jones, Jacqueline. *Labor of Love, Labor of Sorrow: Black Women, Work, and the Family from Slavery to the Present.* New York: Basic Books, 1985.

Kolchin, Peter. *American Slavery, 1619–1877.* New York: Hill and Wang, 1993.

Levine, Lawrence W. *Black Culture and Black Consciousness: Afro-American Folk Thought from Slavery to Freedom.* New York: Oxford University Press, 1977.

Litwack, Leon. *Been in the Storm So Long.* New York: Alfred A. Knopf, 1979.

McDaniel, George W. *Hearth and Home: Preserving a People's Culture.* Philadelphia: Temple University Press, 1982.

Meier, August, and Rudwick, Elliot. *From Plantation to Ghetto.* Third edition. New York: Hill and Wang, 1976.

Mellon, James, ed. *Bullwhip Days: The Slaves Remember.* New York: Avon Books, 1988.

Morgan, Edmund. *American Slavery, American Freedom.* New York: W. W. Norton, 1975.

Owens, Leslie. *This Species of Property: Slave Life and Culture in the Old South.* New York: Oxford University Press, 1976.

Raboteau, Albert J. *Slave Religion: The "Invisible Institution" in the Antebellum South.* New York: Oxford University Press, 1978.

Starobin, Robert S., and Berlin, Ira, eds. *Blacks in Bondage: Letters of American Slaves.* Second edition. New York: Wiener, 1988.

Vlach, John Michael. *Back of the Big House: The Architecture of Plantation Slavery.* Chapel Hill: University of North Carolina Press, 1993.

White, Deborah Gray. *Arn't I a Woman? Female Slaves in the Plantation South.* New York: W. W. Norton, 1985.

INDEX

ACKNOWLEDGMENTS

Photographs and illustrations used by permission from the Penn School Collection, permission granted by Penn Center, Inc., St. Helena Island, South Carolina: pp. 2, 46; Brown Brothers: pp. 6, 7, 67, 71; Library of Virginia: pp. 8, 39 (right); IPS: p. 12 (top); Corbis-Bettmann: pp. 12 (bottom), 15, 16, 18, 20, 23 (bottom), 24, 29, 31, 35, 36, 43, 44 (bottom), 48, 50, 56, 61, 64, 68, 70, 75, 78, 82; courtesy of the Peabody Essex Museum, Salem, Massachusetts: p. 14; Library of Congress: pp. 23 (top), 47, 52, 54, 58, 79, 83; Sophia Smith Collection, Smith College: p. 25; courtesy of the North Carolina Division of Archives and History: p. 26; Missouri Historical Society, St. Louis: p. 28; Chicago Historical Society: p. 40; © Collection of The New-York Historical Society: p. 44 (top); National Archives (W&C 112): p. 73; Archive Photos: pp. 39 (left), 69, 72, 76 (both), 80.

Front cover: Courtesy of the North Carolina Division of Archives and History
Back cover: Archive Photos
Cover design by Michael Tacheny

LERNER'S AWARD-WINNING PEOPLE'S HISTORY SERIES:

Buffalo Gals: Women of the Old West

Dressed for the Occasion: What Americans Wore 1620-1970

Farewell, John Barleycorn: Prohibition in the United States

Get Up and Go: The History of American Road Travel

Just What the Doctor Ordered: The History of American Medicine

Slave Young, Slave Long: The American Slave Experience

Snapshot: America Discovers the Camera

This Land Is Your Land: The American Conservation Movement

Uncle Sam Wants You: The Military Men and Women of World War II

V Is for Victory: The American Home Front during World War II

We Have Marched Together: The Working Children's Crusade

When This Cruel War Is Over: The Civil War Home Front

For more information, please call 1-800-328-4929 or visit www.lernerbooks.com.